From Under
a Rock

A Christian Woman's
Experience with,
and Healing from,
Depression

Colleen Simms Duncan

ISBN 978-1-0980-8229-1 (paperback)
ISBN 978-1-0980-8230-7 (digital)

Christian Faith Publishing, Inc.
832 Park Avenue
Meadville, PA 16335
www.christianfaithpublishing.com

Printed in the United States of America

3

Pictures are from the following people:

ARL (Alysha Long)
Tara T (Tara Tralee Fitzpatrick)
SF (Shannon Fitzpatrick)
EF (Eric Foster)

Disclaimer

I am not a trained psychologist or psychotherapist, nor do I have a degree in any type of counseling. I am just an ordinary person who has struggled, as far back as I can remember, with depression and low self-esteem.

Even successes in my life did not prevent me from thinking I was a failure. I have an associate degree of science in radiology, I am a licensed vocational nurse, and I was ordained as a minister, but none of that lifted me above depression. I love to write poetry and songs, I play a few musical instruments (somewhat), and I always considered these hobbies my therapy.

The battle with depression and low self-esteem is real. It's painful. And it can be deadly. It is my hope that anyone experiencing depression or low self-esteem who reads my story will realize there is hope, and healing is possible.

I dedicate this work of heart to my husband, Don, who is my emotional support no matter what and gives me the love and the freedom to grow and heal even when he doesn't understand what is going on inside me.

Nancy Rai Quillen, my best friend, who proofread the first three chapters and told me, "No changes. You have to finish this." Sadly, she passed away before I did. I miss her. I think this finished project would have made her proud. At least I like to think so.

ARL

Prologue

I was stunned when the pastor's wife approached me after church and asked me to sing the special on the following Sunday, but I slapped a quick smile on my face and said, "Sure!" Quickly ducking out of the church before anyone had a chance to stop and chat with me, I tried to hold back the storm of emotions assaulting my heart and my mind.

Just four months earlier, my father placed a gun to his head, pulled the trigger, and ended his life, and now I'm supposed to sing the Father's Day special! What in the world was I supposed to sing, "Faith of Our Fathers, Living Still"? Oh yeah, that would work, I thought sarcastically.

Three days before Father's Day, after sorting through all my backup tapes, sheet music, and songbooks, I was still at a loss. While praying for God to tell me what to do, I remembered a poem I wrote in memory of my father two months after his death. That poem would be appropriate, but I had no melody for it.

As I continued to pray for God's help, I thought of the men and women at the county jail where I sang and lead Bible studies on Tuesday nights. I thought of their stories, of how alone they felt sometimes, some abandoned by their own friends and families, and how much it meant to them to be hugged or prayed for, to know someone cared for them whether they were innocent or guilty. My love for them put a melody in my heart. And on Father's Day, after sharing with the congregation how the song came about, I sang my new song about my *heavenly* Father. There were few dry eyes in the church that morning.

After the service, the pastor's wife—eyes red from crying—came up to me and apologized for what she had done. I told her how glad I was that she did, for it turned out to be a great day of healing for me as God revealed to me, yet again, that even in our darkest moments, He holds us in the palm of His hands and never ever leaves us. Amen.

(Just a few short months away, this important lesson would help me survive an even greater tragedy than I could ever have imagined.)

I Will Hold You

1. Alone in my room, I cried out to God, "Where are You?
    I don't feel You around."
    He said, "Rest, My child, you're in the palm of My hand,
    And never will I let you down."

Chorus
    "In the palm of My hand I will hold you;
    I will shield you with My wing.
    And one day I will carry you up to My throne
    Where the saints and the angels sing."

2. Sometimes when my life is clouded with strife,
    At each turn, the devil strikes me.
    My Father says, "Peace, child, just remember Me now,
    For I am much greater than he."

No Rest for the Weary

The sound of crunching gravel woke me up with a start. Once again, I had fallen asleep driving home from work. I jerked the steering wheel to get back onto the asphalt, my heart beating like a drum.

For months now, I had struggled to stay awake while driving. The sound of crunching gravel was becoming quite a familiar sound. One time, the loud blast of a car horn woke me, and I realized I was in the wrong lane, facing oncoming traffic. Thankfully, I was able to swerve back into my lane without causing an accident. Even drinking coffee or ice water (which always worked before) could not keep me awake. Being startled awake by hot coffee or ice water hitting my lap was becoming a regular, frightening, and worrisome experience.

Even more alarming, I struggled frequently to stay awake at work at a job I dearly loved. I enjoyed the interaction with patients and everything about x-ray technology, but as soon as there was a break between patients, I would struggle fiercely to keep the sandman at bay. Sometimes I even fell asleep for an instant in the middle of a sentence while talking to my coworkers. I could see the concern or confusion in their faces and hear it in the tone of their voices. I'm surprised I wasn't asked by management to take a drug test. There were no drugs. I seldom even took an over-the-counter medication for a headache.

I looked forward to going home so I could sleep, knowing sleep was not likely to come any time soon. As difficult as it was to stay awake while driving or working, it was equally difficult to sleep once I arrived home. I hit the bed totally drained and watched the hands of the clock slowly make its rounds hour after hour, the ticking of the clock seemingly amplified in the quiet of the night. Around 4:00 a.m., I would finally drift off to sleep, only to jerk awake an hour or two later, unable to determine what had disturbed me. Rarely did I fall back to sleep.

The fatigue was unbearable. I thought about being admitted to the hospital so I could get some sleep, but I worked at a hospital, so I knew that was a ridiculous thought. Every couple of hours, vital signs are checked, medications are administered, and there is constant noise (chatter between nurses, phones ringing, medical equipment being moved or in use, etc.).

My exhausted mind and body were not going to be able to take much more. At this point, I began to wonder if I was dying—but I didn't think so—or if I was ill and just didn't recognize with what.

Bad Attitude

"SHUT UP! I DON'T CARE! GO AWAY! LEAVE ME ALONE! PLEASE LEAVE ME THE HECK ALONE!" I screamed in my mind as I took another call from yet another person wanting to talk about his/her problems to someone who cared. Normally, I DID care, but for some reason I didn't understand, hearing another person's problems was now far too heavy and draining on me, sucking the air and life right out of me. I couldn't bear it. I unwillingly listened (sometimes holding the phone away from my ear) and offered few words of comfort or advice while struggling to keep from screaming at them to leave me alone. I began to avoid answering the phone. I was so afraid I would finally lose control and start screaming at the caller. Since no one close to me knew the turmoil I was going through, any outburst would have been a total shock to them. I hoped what I was going through was temporary and would end soon before I lost control and said something that would cause emotional injuries I may not be able to mend.

Always able to find something positive about life before and finding joy in making people smile, I found myself now with no energy, no zest for life, no desire to do ANYTHING (especially being around other people), and dreading to get out of bed in the morning to face another day.

I did not share what was happening to me with anyone because I didn't know what was going on inside me. I couldn't explain it, but I knew I couldn't keep on like this for much longer. Something had to give.

Dying?

Several years earlier, my physician told me I was dying and probably had a year, at most, to live. I wasn't surprised because I felt the "dying process" going on in my body as I steadily lost weight and got weaker and weaker.

Just a few days before that appointment with my doctor, I felt an incredible pain in my head as my daughter and I were leaving church. It felt like my brain was trying to explode as the pressure and pain increased. Pulling through a church parking lot at the end of the morning service, I realized there was a group of teenagers ahead of me. Since they weren't moving, I began to try to stomp on the brake but couldn't remember which of the two pedals was the correct one. I kept stomping on the floorboard, afraid I would stomp on the wrong pedal and run the kids down. My daughter began screaming.

The next thing I was conscious of was my car bumping into something. As I lifted my head to see how many kids I had hit, I realized that, somehow, I had made it home. By the grace of God, I made it the mile home down a busy street, crossing under a free-way overpass, zigzagging through the apartment parking lot, until I struck the curb in front of my apartment. My terrified, crying daughter, not understanding what was going on, jumped out of the car, ran up the stairs and into our apartment. Later, my physician told me he believed I'd had a stroke. (I didn't go to the doctor until a month later because I was waiting for my insurance to kick in and didn't have the money to get the medical care that I obviously needed).

Now, many years later, whatever was happening was different. Although I felt physically and emotionally "dead," I didn't have the sensation of dying as I did in the previous event. I caught myself often gasping for air after holding my breath without realizing I was doing so. It was almost as if the very act of breathing was too difficult.

The only time I felt any comfort was at night as I lay listening to my husband's gentle breathing as he slept. At those times I felt safe, sheltered. But away from him in the quiet of the night, I felt devastated, crushed, and alone even though I knew in my spirit God was ever present. Only my strong work ethic, love for my family, and sense of responsibility to my family and God kept me motivated to do the things I had to do each day.

One night, I realized I had to figure out what was going on and deal with whatever my problem was. I had to find a solution before everything I held dear was destroyed. I thought of going to the doctor, but how could I explain something I didn't understand? I finally decided to sit down at my first opportunity and make a list of all my "symptoms" to see if I could figure it out. When I did, I was totally surprised at the outcome.

The "Symptoms"

As I considered my "symptoms," I tried to categorize them and ended up with six main categories:

1. Constant fatigue
    a) Difficulty staying awake during my waking hours
    b) Insomnia during my sleeping hours
2. Bad attitude
    a) Anger, frustration for no apparent reason
    b) Annoyance with anything or anyone that required my attention
    c) An "I don't care" reaction to others' problems
3. Physical weakness (Besides being tired from lack of sleep, I felt weak.)
4. Emotional numbness (This presented when I was not angry, frustrated, or annoyed.)
5. Loss of appetite
6. Incohesive thinking
    a) Unable to concentrate.
    b) Unable to keep thoughts orderly even while praying.
    c) No matter what I started thinking about, if I tried to think for very long, my thoughts ended up at the same painful place.

I read over my list several times. As no physical symptoms other than fatigue from lack of sleep manifested, I was pretty sure I was not physically ill. Again, I read the list, and this time, the last phrase jumped out at me—"the same painful place." I was suffering from depression! All my life, from the age of four, I struggled off and on with different intensities of depression. So why hadn't I recognized it? I believe it was because this depression was so much deeper than I had ever experienced before that I had kept its source suppressed.

Now that I knew what I was dealing with, I had to root out the cause, face it, and find a way to heal.

"Depressed Little Child"

On a recent shopping trip, my mom made the comment, "You were always a depressed little child. I think only Puff understood you." I was stunned. I never knew my mom was aware of my depression.

I smiled at the memory of the little white dog (a spitz-cocker spaniel mix). When she came into my life, she was a tiny bundle of white fur with big brown eyes and a fan-shaped tail. We named her Powder Puff Simms and considered her a big part of our family.

Sometimes I would sit on the front porch, engulfed in depression, crying, and worrying about what would happen to me if my parents ever divorced or I was orphaned or kidnapped. I thought I would have to choose one parent over another in the event of a divorce and knew I would run away because I could not hurt either parent by doing that. Thankfully, none of those things ever happened, but I made my plans just in case.

Puff seemed to understand my distress, and as my tears fell, she would whine and put her head in my lap as if to comfort me. (I'm pretty sure I saw tears in her eyes sometimes too.) Once I stopped crying, she would trot off to do her daily hunt, looking back at me to make sure I was okay before going on into the tall grasses in the fields behind our house, where she loved to hunt for rabbit. I don't know if she ever caught one, but she sure enjoyed the chase.

I often wondered what it would be like to have a human friend like that—one who cared for and understood me.

One day, my only friend was gone. She had several litters of puppies over the years, and my dad got tired of it, so he put her in the car and dropped her off somewhere. I was devastated and so very alone. Now I had no one to talk to, to shed my tears with, no one who could understand me. I never felt so alone in my life.

During all my school years, I had occasional friends, but none that I allowed to get really close to me (except one, and she moved after one year in my elementary class). Without Puff, I just bottled up all my pain and loneliness.

The Start of Childhood Depression and Shame

There is, and always has been, great debate on whether nature or nurture plays the biggest role in depression. The term nurture indicates, to me, how one has been raised, but I believe life experiences should be included within the scope of nurture as one's experiences in and out of the home help form who you are.

Several people on my father's side of the family suffered from depression and more than one committed suicide. My grandmother drank lye and died a very painful death. My father said she was suffering from several large stomach tumors that were causing her great pain and that he was finally able to convince her to have surgery. According to my dad, the pain she suffered after surgery was just too much for her to bear, so she ended it in a desperate and horrible action. Dad forever blamed himself for her death. I was told my great grandmother killed herself also, but I don't know that for sure.

I already mentioned my dad's suicide, so heredity probably did play a huge role in my emotional instability, but so I believe did my life experiences.

When I was four years old, my family and I lived in a little house next to a fenced-in park. My mother could barely see me as I played there with the neighbors, but she felt I was safe because of the fence, and we knew the kids I was playing with.

One day, a boy asked me if I wanted to play cowboys and Indians with him and his girl cousin. I agreed, but as soon as they tied me to a tree, I sensed something wasn't right. The boy's demeanor had changed. The look on his face frightened me.

They began to sexually assault me with the boy directing the girl what to do to me. I remember the bark of the tree biting into my skin as I tried to pull my body inside the tree to escape the terrible pain I was feeling. I thought of God but didn't call out to Him to help me because I didn't want Him to see my shame.

Suddenly, the boy said to his cousin, "Here comes her dad. Untie her and let her go." When she untied me, the boy instructed me to run. I ran straight to the swing set where I knew I could quickly climb up high to feel safe. Not knowing what had happened to me, my dad was angry when I didn't come when he called, but I was too afraid to move. Dad pulled me down off the swing set and whipped me all the way home. As there was blood in my underwear, it was apparent to my mom that those kids had hurt me. When she brought it up to my dad, he chose to let it go, probably because those kids were the grandchildren of our landlord.

I trusted my father, so I never questioned his reaction. I believed, somehow, what happened was my fault. I was confused, afraid, and ashamed. That is the way I felt for the next couple of decades. I tried very hard not to bring any more shame to my dad in the years to come.

Damages

At four years of age, I believed I should die, that I was a shame and a burden to my father, but it was a couple of years later that I decided to take my own life. I considered jumping from a moving car, ingesting poison, stabbing or shooting myself, hanging myself, etc. Since I was too young to have a realistic concept of death, the only thing that kept me from carrying out my plan was fear of my father. If I tried to kill myself and failed, my dad would punish me and would be stuck taking care of an invalid. My actions would bring even more shame and disappointment to him. I couldn't bear to see the shame on his face as he took care of his invalid daughter, so I waited.

The thoughts of suicide continued with me into my adulthood, and I finally made a serious attempt in my midtwenties. Thankfully, I was unsuccessful and ended up with a wrecked car, busted lip from hitting the steering wheel, bruised ribs, bruised legs, and a lot of pain, but no serious injury. I lived three hundred miles from my dad, so it wasn't likely he would ever find out.

I needed psychiatric counseling. But in those days, there was a stigma attached to people who went to psychiatrists, and one could even be refused a job if there was a record of psychiatric care.

Because I never talked to anyone about my depression, no one knew I needed help. My mom suspected I needed counseling of some type in my teen years, but my dad blew it off like he did with any problem he couldn't solve himself or didn't agree with, and my mom didn't pursue it because of her fear of him. Dad had a serious drinking problem and was not a fun person to be around when he was drunk. He became angry and controlling. Even his brother tried not to set him off when he was drinking.

Bad Seed

A few years later, Mom, Dad, and I were watching a movie called *The Bad Seed*. In this movie, a beautiful little blond-haired girl caused the death of a little boy she was jealous of and that of a nice man that knew what she had done. I asked my dad what "bad seed" meant. He said some people, for reasons no one understood, were just born bad seed. The way he looked at me when he said it led me to think he was telling me that I was bad seed, and that's why bad things happened to me. Of course, it was all in my imagination, but I didn't know that at the time.

I was determined not to bring any more shame to my family but wasn't sure how I was going to accomplish that if I was bad seed. I also determined to never let anyone else know the truth about me (or at least what I thought was the truth).

I so desperately wanted people to love me, but I was afraid of letting anyone too close. They might find out I was bad seed and not associate with me anymore. Shutting myself off to close relationships made me so lonely.

When I was seventeen, I was raped by someone I knew. Remembering my dad's reaction when I was four, I knew three things:

1. He would blame me because it had to be my fault.
2. I would bring more shame upon my family.
3. My dad would lose his terrible temper and would probably shoot and kill my attacker (not to protect me but because of the dishonor the attacker brought on our family name).

If my dad ended up in prison, it would be my fault. If I told my mom, she would just sit and cry and not know what to do. My mom had been raised in a loving, nurturing home and had no idea how to deal with emotional problems like mine. She cared, she just wouldn't know what to do, so she would just cry. I felt trapped, alone in my pain and shame.

Several months later, the pressure of holding all my emotions inside caused me to break down. I remember only bits and pieces of that moment. I remember arguing with my mom (probably started by me), then standing in front of my mom, weakly beating on her chest, crying hysterically and screaming, "I hate you! I hate you!" She thought I was screaming at her, but I was actually screaming at myself.

It broke my heart when I heard her say, "I'm sorry you feel that way." For some reason, I couldn't seem to tell her the truth, that I was screaming at myself.

I must have collapsed because the next thing I remember, I was on my bed screaming and crying. I heard someone ask what was wrong with me, but I couldn't hear the answer, and I don't remember anything else about that event.

Of course, just as with the playground incident, I was not taken to a doctor. Some people would be appalled about this, but I never blamed my parents for not taking me to get help. These were different times. Like so many of my peers, we didn't even go to our family physician except to get vaccines required for school or for emergencies.

Failures

A few months after I graduated high school, I became engaged to a nice young man. Realizing I wasn't emotionally ready for marriage, I finally told him I wanted to wait. It didn't go over very well as he believed I must have found someone else, another man. No matter how hard I tried, I couldn't get him to understand I just wasn't ready. Finally, in fear of losing him, I agreed to set a date, and seven months later, we married.

Seven years and two precious sons later, we divorced. This was followed by two more failed marriages.

First, I married an alcoholic who beat me until I ended up with nerve damage on the left side of my brain. Like many victims of spousal abuse, I stayed long after I should have left because he threatened to kill my family. I believed him. But one night after a particularly vicious beating, I found myself standing over his drunken, passed-out body with a skillet in one hand and a shotgun in the other. As I tried to decide whether to bash his knees in so he could feel the pain he had been pouring out on me or just put a bullet in his head so he couldn't hurt me anymore, the reality of what I was about to do hit me hard. I was about to stoop as low as him, and I would probably end up in prison. I put my weapons up, but the next incident made me realize I had to find a way to escape.

A little over a year after we married, I became pregnant. He did not want children, and I didn't believe in abortion. So I tried to hide the pregnancy until it was too late for him to do anything about it. I never gained much during my pregnancies until the last couple of months, so he didn't realize I was pregnant until I was 5 1/2 months along.

When kicking me in the stomach with steel-toed boots didn't cause me to lose the baby, he made an appointment for me with a Planned Parenthood clinic. My husband put a shotgun in the pickup with us so I would remember he was serious about not wanting a baby. I believed his threats and went with him to the clinic, thinking, somehow, I would get them to help me.

Once out of my husband's earshot, I tried to tell the doctor and the nurse I didn't want the abortion. I thought they would help me escape. I also thought that once they saw how far along I was, they would tell my husband they wouldn't do it. (Obviously, I was quite naive.)

I was afraid to just leave without anyone helping me because I knew there was a shotgun in the truck, and he WOULD use it. I think the nurse just thought I was afraid of having the abortion because she told me it wouldn't hurt much and started the procedure. She lied. I felt like she was ripping me apart inside. Afterward, my blood pressure dropped very low. I felt like if I moved, I would pass out. The nurse took my blood pressure and asked me if I was still alive. I just looked at her.

As soon as I was stable, my husband loaded me in the car, drove to my job, and dropped me off!

Escape

Not long after the abortion, I began to have nightmares about a little girl, approximately three or four years old. In one dream, she was walking down a plank sidewalk, like in the old Westerns, hand in hand with a mortician who was dressed all in black with a black top hat. In my dream, I was walking behind them. She turned, looked at me, and said, "Why did you let them kill me?" I woke up sobbing each time, and the nightmare was always the same.

Drugs became my escape from the nightmares and the guilt it caused me. How I held down a job during this time of my life, I don't know because I did drugs daily (to avoid nightmares at night and to stay awake at work). I also took up smoking cigarettes to help me stay awake and to cut down on how much marijuana I was smoking. By the time I quit, I was smoking three packs a day and coughing blood.

In my mind, I had gone from being bad seed to being a chain-smoking drug addict and baby killer. It didn't matter that I had been taken to the clinic against my will and forced to go through with the abortion at the threat of the death of my family and myself if I didn't. I knew that if I had left him in time, the baby and I would have stood a chance.

When I finally decided to escape from him, I knew I would end up dead trying if I wasn't successful. It was a few weeks after I decided to leave that I finally actually got up the nerve to do it.

One day while my husband was at work, I grabbed a small suitcase and began to pack. "What if he comes home and catches me? I'm dead!" I thought. Shaking in fear, I quickly scribbled him a note and dashed out of the apartment. Afraid of being caught with a suitcase in my hand, I didn't make it farther than the bushes surrounding the apartment complex.

From the safety of the bushes, I watched as my husband returned home from work. A couple of minutes later, he stormed out of the apartment, jumped into his pickup, and sped out of the parking lot. Afraid it was a trick and that he would return soon, I stayed frozen in my spot in the bushes. Apparently, I was right because in a very short time, I saw him stealthily approach the apartment. His pickup was nowhere in sight. He had parked it a couple of blocks away and walked back thinking I would return to the apartment for my things if I thought he was away.

Unaware of what was going on, a neighbor approached our apartment with a cup in her hand, obviously to borrow sugar or something else she needed. My husband jerked the door open and startled the neighbor so that she stepped back. I watched her hold out the cup and say something to my husband. He took the cup and went off to get what she needed. In the process, he left the door open. The neighbor poked her head in and look around, and once she had her cup in hand, she thanked him and quickly returned to her apartment.

A few minutes later, cops surrounded the apartment with guns drawn. They knocked on the door, which was opened to them by a very startled, angry man.

Even with the police there, I was too terrified to approach for several minutes. Once they cuffed my husband and brought him outside to sit on the sidewalk while they checked the apartment, I finally came out of the bushes.

Although I had bruises all over my face and neck from being hit and choked, I had no serious injuries. Unknown to me, when the police arrived, they found the apartment covered with blood (even flung all over the walls), pottery shattered on the floor, and everything in complete disarray as if a violent struggle had occurred there. The bathroom door was closed when they arrived, and one officer told me that until they opened that door, they were convinced they were about to find my body in the bathtub.

I was shaking so hard as I approached I think I was about to pass out. The officers had me sit down and explained they had received a call from the neighbor who came to borrow sugar. She told them that when she poked her head inside the apartment, she saw blood all over the walls, floor, and furniture and that she was sure he had killed me. Many of the neighbors knew of his temper when he was drinking, which was often, and they were afraid of him too.

For example, when I was going to nursing school, one of the neighbors made a vulgar comment to me as I walked to my car in my nursing uniform. I made a smart remark back. When I returned from school, there was a knock on my door. Three of my neighbors were standing there and asked to use my phone. I let them in, not thinking anything about it because they were friends of my husband and often used our phone. Suddenly, one of them pulled out a large butcher knife.

"What are you doing?" I asked.

Obviously nervous, they stood close together between me and the front door. One of them said, "We're here to shut you up before you tell your husband what we said."

Although I was very scared, I was also very angry. And when I'm angry I react. I said, "Whichever one of you [and I won't say what I called them here because I don't talk that way anymore] wants to go first, come on because one or more of you is going to go down with me!"

Totally stunned at my reaction, they just stood there looking at me for a minute. Finally, one of them said, "We don't want no trouble."

I said, "Then you better put your knife away, or you're going to get trouble. I fight my own fights, and I don't fight words with weapons. You insulted me this morning with words, and I said words back. I thought it was over. But if you don't think it is, come on. Your choice. Bring it on or leave."

Crazy as it seems, they actually discussed it. Once they decided leaving was the best option, they asked me what I was going to tell my husband. I said, "I told you I fight my own fights." Thankfully, they decided to leave.

When my husband got home, I told him what happened, and to my shock, he just laughed. He thought it was terribly funny.

On the day I hid in the bushes, while the police were still at our apartment, I did finally leave. And a few weeks later, he DID try to find my family. I received a nervous phone call from one of my neighbors saying she saw him driving around the block looking for me, but he apparently couldn't remember which house was my parents' home, so he left. He was probably drunk, and I knew he had his loaded rifle with him. I never saw or heard from him again.

Slow to learn, I married again. I gave birth to two more children—another awesome son and a beautiful blue-eyed daughter. This marriage also ended in divorce, but out of love and respect for my children, I will not share the details of the two marriages in which I was blessed with them.

Self-Esteem

Obviously, I had self-esteem issues. I was "bad seed" and a failure at marriage and life in general. The only place I felt I had any worth was at church. Church had always been an integral part of my life. My parents made sure that from the date of my birth, I was in church.

By the time I was thirteen, I was teaching vacation Bible school every summer, singing in the adult choir, and at sixteen, I was teaching in Sunday school. I taught the Girls' Auxiliary, which teaches young girls to memorize scriptures and how to work in mission fields. My sister and her best friend were in my group. As a big sister, I loved getting to tell my little sister what to do and give her and her friend assignments which I got to check over when they turned them in. The church my family and I attended was a small mission church with limited resources of people willing to teach. And since I was willing and able, I was allowed to teach at a young age. I poured myself into it and loved every minute of it. Even at church, I was afraid people would find out about the real me, and I would lose my place there too. So I was very careful to be the "nice Christian girl" they thought I was.

Away from church, I felt like I was useless and just taking up space, that I was worthless and would never amount to anything. Low self-esteem fed my depression like bears feed on honey.

Good Comes My Way

While attending church with my mother one Sunday, I met the love of my life. When he originally called me and asked me out, I told him I wasn't dating but that I would meet him for lunch.

A couple of weeks before Don called me, a lady I worked with asked me when I was going to start dating again. She said I was too young to waste myself without a man. I couldn't figure out how she thought I was wasting myself just because I didn't have a man in my life. I told her I had proven to myself I was too stupid to choose wisely and that I was better off being by myself. She thought I was nuts and told me so. She asked, "If there is a man out there for you, what would be your requirements?" I said he would have to be mentally, monetarily (so I couldn't be blamed for financial problems anymore), and spiritually secure. She thought I was being unrealistic. I told her if God had anyone out there for me, He would have to hog-tie me and drag me to him because I would be screaming and running the other way.

When Don called me for a date, I agreed to meet him for lunch because, knowing him from church, I was aware he met all my requirements. I still didn't intend more than just a couple of lunch meetings (not dates), but six months later, we married, and he proved to be all I dreamed of. We've been married now over twenty-two years, and I'm still glad I decided to meet him for lunch.

Don was (and still is) a great source of strength for me even though he didn't understand my constant fear and the battles with depression. He never put me down or acted like I was being stupid because of my unrealistic level of fear. I felt so guilty struggling against fear all the time because I knew that the Bible says that fear is not of God. Unlike other Christians who criticized me for the fear and depression, Don accepted me as I was (and still does) without judgment and gave me the space to heal and grow. He never criticizes me and has a very kind way of letting me know when I'm getting off track. He is so calm and takes almost everything in stride, whereas I tend to get all bent out of shape when things are going wrong. I should take some lessons from him.

Hell Breaks In

Eighteen months after my dad's suicide, Don and I were having dinner with friends from church in their home. There was a knock at the door, and to my surprise, my youngest son stood there. Our friends invited him in, and it was obvious, immediately, that something was wrong.

With lips quivering and with a choked voice, he said, "It's Kelly." I began bombarding him with questions while he struggled to maintain his composure. "Is he all right? Was he in an accident? Is he hurt bad? Where is he? Is he in the hospital?" With each question, I could see the difficulty my son was having. I knew it was hard on him, but I HAD to know. Finally, since he didn't seem to be able to answer my questions, I knew. Kelly was gone. All the air went out of me as I voiced my realization that Kelly was dead. My son nodded.

Even as I asked my son all those questions, I felt guilty putting him through that, but I had to know. I would have done the same thing for any of my children.

I don't remember much after that. I remember getting into the car. I don't remember returning home. I remember not having any strength even to move and only doing what I had to. I remember getting up on Sunday morning and telling my family we had to go to church so others would know that no matter what had happened, God still is. I think everyone was stunned when we showed up. After the service, I went up to the front. I didn't have the strength to go up where the guest speaker was, so I asked if I could just stay down at floor level. He said yes and brought me a mike. I told the congregation that regardless of what happened, God is still God.

Losing Kelly was the worst thing I had ever experienced. He was such a ray of sunshine wherever he was. He played football but giggled like a girl. Sometimes, out of the clear blue, he would start giggling over a joke everyone else had already forgotten about and that would start the rest of us laughing all over again. He played guitar and was quite an artist. Most of all, he was my son. He was part of me.

Kelly loved to make people laugh and bring them joy. He hated hurting or disappointing people. Even his "teenage rebellion" only lasted a couple of weeks. He said the guilt he felt during this time wasn't worth it.

One day all that joy was snuffed out when problems he was facing in his life became, in his mind, insurmountable. I don't know what all the issues were that he was dealing with because he was a very private person and didn't want others worrying about him, but he came over one day, crying, and said he'd made a mess of things. He'd made some wrong decisions trying to ease his pain when he couldn't seem to fix the problem. These actions backfired and caused him and others more pain.

I could see how crushed he was and tried to get him to stay with me a few days and let me help him get professional counseling, but he said he couldn't stay and that he had to go back home. I was afraid for him to leave, but I couldn't make him stay.

That was the last time I saw him alive. Three days later, he was found in his car in the garage with the engine running. He'd left a note. The only two words I remember are "LIFE SUCKS." This is from someone who'd spent his life making people smile.

Life after Kelly

As I lay in bed at night, scripture verses ran through my mind, "He will never leave you, nor forsake you." Although I knew He was there, I couldn't feel His presence.

"The joy of the Lord is your strength" (Nehemiah 8:10). Joy seemed to be just beyond my reach. I knew it was there but couldn't tap into it.

"Believing, you rejoice with joy unspeakable and full of glory" (1 Peter 1:8). I wanted to feel that joy, but my hurt was so deep.

"Weeping may endure for the night, but joy comes in the morning" (Psalms 30:5). Oh God, when will that morning come? When will I feel Your joy again?

Night after night I felt dead, broken, weak. Night after night, tears spent, I prayed for God's joy to replace the horrible grief and pain in my heart. I knew joy would come once I was able to lift my head out of the ocean of grief I was drowning in.

One night it finally happened. After more hours of crying, hurting, and praying, the peace and joy finally broke through, and my soul overflowed. A song came into my heart and mind, and I began to tell my husband all about my new song, babbling nonstop and at high speed. I noticed my husband kept looking over my shoulder, so I turned to see what he was looking at. The clock! It was 3:00 a.m.! I said, "Oh, I'm sorry." He suggested I get up and write the words down before I forgot them.

That's exactly what I did while my husband went instantly back to sleep. The song is called "The Spirit's Moving." The first verse and chorus were already in my head, and the rest came quickly. I sat at the piano and wrote the words down as I figured out what the keys were. Although Kelly's loss was still very painful, I had finally rejoined the land of the living—for a while.

The Spirit's Moving

Chorus:

The Spirit's moving in my soul since Jesus Christ has made me whole;
No shadow now can dim His brilliant light.
The darkness has been chased away; my Savior has come here to stay;
He's taken all that's wrong and made it right.

1. Glory to the Son of God; all praise is due His name.
    I've been washed in Jesus's blood; I'll never be the same.

2. I have found true peace within, a peace I've never known;
    Joy and love are also mine since I've become His own.

3. Glory to the Son of God who paid the debt for me;
    In my mansion He has built, I'll live eternally.

Success Is Not Enough

Over the next few years, life went on, and I had some successes to be proud of. First, I went back to college and earned an associate degree in science in radiology. I loved radiology, but after several months, I decided I wanted more one-on-one with the patients than I experienced in radiology. Although I continued to work as a radiology technologist, I went back to college and became a licensed vocational nurse. I loved this job too and enjoyed caring for patients and loved them as if they were part of my family (well, most of them). Working as a nurse at a retirement center and at a hospital as an x-ray technologist, I had the best of both worlds.

Several months after I obtained my licenses, I began suffering the "symptoms." Once I realized I was suffering from a very deep depression, I knew I needed help. I considered going to a counselor but had seen other people seem worse after counseling or becoming reliant on medications. Antidepressants would simply cover the result of the depression and not help me root out the cause. (There are good, qualified counselors out there, but I was afraid to take the chance of finding one.)

Next, I considered finding a friend to listen to me and help me work through it, but I'd seen my mom's well-meaning friends unwittingly drag her down into a deeper depression by their sympathy and unwise advice.

Praying and reading Scriptures daily, I began reviewing all the hurts in my life, searching for the cause of my pain. Suddenly one day, with the aid of my "symptoms" list, it hit me like a load of bricks. For years, I'd tried to be everybody else's emotional strength and had never allowed myself to fully grieve over Kelly. Years before, God had helped me over a roadblock by giving me a song that put joy in my heart, but I had never returned to that moment to complete the grieving process. I had never allowed myself to "grieve out." That doesn't mean there is no more grief. It just means I faced the pain head on so that it no longer drains the life out of me or controls me. I had to allow the tears of grief to flow unhindered so they could wash away the rawness of my heart's wound and allow my heart to start to heal. Do I still have tears for Kelly at times? Yes, of course. But the pain is no longer suffocating or paralyzing.

Ignoring or avoiding dealing with an emotional pain is like ignoring a physical wound. If it's not cared for, it can become infected, can spread, and sometimes cause death. (I remember right after Kelly died, the pain I felt led me to understand how someone can grieve themselves to death.)

I wonder sometimes how many people we see on the streets or deal with at work or school are emotionally paralyzed because they have not dealt with an emotional pain or loss. I know one man who lost his wife in a house fire and was so devastated he just walked away, leaving his children for others to care for. No one knew where he was for about thirty years. He finally faced his pain at a downtown mission. The last time I saw him, he was a minister at that same mission and was in the process of reuniting with his grown children.

There will always be sadness over Kelly's absence. He brought so much laughter into the lives of people who knew him. Sometimes there are still tears that fall when I see or hear things that remind me of him, but now the pain doesn't send me into a deep, dark abyss. My memory of Kelly is sweet and brings more smiles than tears now. The image of him making the angels laugh at his silly giggles makes ME laugh.

I thank God for him and look forward to the day when I will see him again. But God will choose that time, not me.

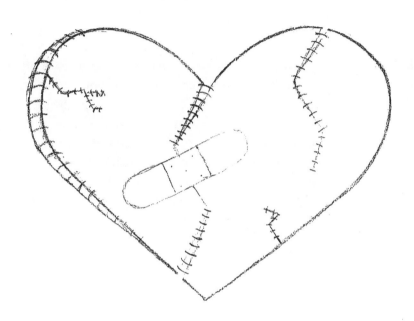

Healing Steps

Healing didn't come until I recognized I had unresolved pain and became willing to face it head on. I couldn't run from it anymore (which I hadn't even realized I was doing until the grief began to mess up my ability to live whole). It was necessary that I recognize I was depressed, recognize the source of the depression, accept that my son was gone from this world, and begin living in my new reality. Without facing reality, there would be no complete healing.

I immersed myself in uplifting Scriptures, set goals instead of just existing every day, and opened up my heart to help other hurting people. There is a lot of healing in helping others who are hurting.

The steps to healing were not easy, but they were clear:

1. Recognize the depression.
2. Acknowledge it.
3. Determine the source.
4. Face it head-on and completely.
5. Move forward and learn to live in your new reality.

An old Chinese proverb says, "The journey of a thousand miles begins with a single step." The first step is the hardest to take, but it can be done. Healing begins with that first step. Just take it one step at a time.

PLEASE NOTE: Sometimes the most discouraging people will be other Christians. I heard "If you had faith, you wouldn't be depressed" instead of "What can I do to help you?" or "I'll be glad to listen if you need to talk" or "Can I pray with you?" The negative, judgmental reactions made me feel guilty and ashamed and made me afraid to ask for help. It hurt me very much at the time, but I realize now they just didn't understand. So instead of being angry, I pray God will tenderize their hearts toward others so they will care even when they don't understand.

Conclusion

When I was deep in depression, I couldn't tap into the joy of the Lord, but I knew He never abandoned me. He held me until I was able to open my heart to all He had ready for me.

Does this mean life is all roses, and I'll never be sad again? Of course not. There will be more losses in my life, but I know, without a doubt, I will never be trapped again in a depression in which I cannot find the way out. Recovery has given me new tools. Other painful events will occur in the future. That's just the way life is. We lose loved ones. We face financial difficulties, health issues, or decisions that will be hard to make. But I know, without a doubt, that no matter what I will face in the future, I WILL BE OKAY.

Notes from the Author

Thanks for taking the time to read this book. I hope and pray that it has helped someone.

Remember, you are never alone. "Yea, though I walk through the valley of the shadow of death, I will fear no evil, for You are with me" (Psalms 23:4). He wants you to be well.

"He heals the brokenhearted and binds up their wounds" (Psalms 147:3). Give Him your heart if you haven't already. He does a better job with it than we do.

"Take My yoke upon you and learn of Me and you will find rest for your souls, for My yoke is easy, and My burden is light" (Matthew 11:29–30).

When I began writing this book, my goal was to give hope to someone struggling with depression and/or the guilt of depression, to encourage someone to take that first step toward healing.

Some parts of this book flowed like water; others took months to write especially when I wrote about my son's death. I realized with each roadblock, there was another step forward I needed to take in my healing. I came through each obstacle stronger and closer than ever to my Lord and to my family. I could have stopped at each road-block, but I am so glad I didn't.

Acknowledgments

I would like to thank my Savior, Jesus Christ, who took my shattered pieces and put me back together and guides me every day even when there are difficult challenges ahead. Without His help, this book would not have been possible.

FROM UNDER A ROCK

About the Author

Colleen, a native of Texas, is a recently retired nurse and x-ray/MRI tech who enjoys spending time with her husband, Don, playing music, and singing at local jams and in bands (not professionally) in Texas and in Branson. They were blessed to play in a gospel group for several years and won three beautiful trophies to place on their mantle. Colleen and Don wrote a few of the songs for the CD the year the band Silver Wings won Texas International Music Association Gospel Group of the year.

Please feel free to contact Colleen Duncan at either address below:
POB 1383   or   POB 806
Boyd TX 76023   Branson MO 65615-0806